GETTING
PROP___
LADDER

How Can Parents and Grandparents Help –
Everything First-Time Buyers Need To Know

Scott Rawlings

POWERHOUSE
— PUBLICATIONS —

COPYRIGHT

Powerhouse Publications
Unit 124. 94 London Road
Headington, Oxford
OX3 9FN

www.powerhousepublishing.com

TESTIMONIALS

"I was impressed by the breakdown – making something very complicated sound simple is not easy!"
– Jenny, London.

"Scott is a mortgage super star!"
– Sara, London.

"Really informative. I found this really helpful."
– Mark, Oxford.

"It provided a good overview for me as a first-time buyer as to the requirements and the process of getting a mortgage."
– Will, Birmingham.

"It was very useful and helpful. It gave me some thought and I will be speaking to my hubby so we may be in touch at a later date."
– Christine, Oxford.

"Very helpful advice."
– Matt, Cheltenham.

"I learnt a lot and found it very interesting."
– Polly, London.

"This was really helpful and I came at a great time as I am currently starting to look at properties."
– Fiona, London.

DEDICATION

This book is dedicated to all the first-time buyers out there. (I was one of those once and know how daunting, but also exciting, it can be). Also, to all the people out there who just want to help their family members. (I will be one of those some day and I think that day will come sooner than I think)…

Contents

Introduction 7

PART 1 9

    1. Guarantor Mortgages..11

    2. Helping with the Deposit 14

    3. How to Fund the Gift or Loan............................18

    4. Equity Release / Lifetime Mortgages....................21

    5. Discounted Family Purchase/Gifting Property 26

    6. Other Considerations 28

    7. Wills..33

PART 2 35

    8. How Much Can I Borrow? 37

    9. Size of Deposit 41

    10. Upfront Costs 44

    11. Monthly Costs 51

    12. Insurances 54

    13. Different Mortgage Options..............................61

    14. Credit Scoring and Searching............................66

    15. Estate Agents..69

    16. Are Some Properties Harder To Arrange Mortgages
        On Than Others? 82

    17. Help To Buy..84

Glossary...101

Acknowledgements..103

Sources 105

About the Author..107

Introduction

Bank of Mum and Dad is a phrase that has appeared in the headlines frequently in the last five years. I'm sure you have heard this phrase before, but would it surprise you to learn that according to a report released this year by Legal & General[1], the total contribution of families and friends to help first-time buyers will have totalled £6.3 billion in 2019. This figure effectively makes Bank of Mum and Dad the eleventh largest mortgage lender in the UK. And would it also surprise you to learn that the government help-to-buy scheme (which I'll be explaining later in this book), despite its success, has helped fewer people to buy than Bank of Mum and Dad?

I meet hundreds, maybe thousands, of first-time buyers every year and the statistics that I am seeing are that at least one in two of those are getting help in some form from a family member. And, rightly or wrongly, it's becoming the norm – especially for millennials facing the daunting task of trying to get on that illusive ladder before they turn 35. The average age for first-time buyers in 2019 was thirty-three. In 2007, it was thirty-one – and I believe this trend of increasing average age is set to continue.

So the question facing many parents, grandparents and family members is: "How can I best help my son, daughter, family member to get on the property ladder?" In this part of the book, I will be explaining the key ways that exist to help financially. In Part 2 of the book, I will run through all the things that I think a first-time buyer needs to know.

I meet lots and lots of first-time buyers and I often hear the phrase, "I

---

[1] https://www.legalandgeneral.com/bank-of-mum-and-dad/bomad-report-2019.pdf

don't know where to start." The idea behind this book is that it's a starting point. It will answer the key questions I get asked by first-time buyers, such as:

- How much can I borrow?
- What deposit do I need?
- What costs do I need to budget for?
- How much does a mortgage cost each month?
- How do I negotiate with agents?
- What government schemes are available to me?

When those questions are answered, buyers can create a plan. That might mean going out and starting to look at properties tomorrow or, indeed, it might mean saving for the next few years knowing the amount you need to save. But it will definitely answer questions and help you to formulate a plan. It's rare that people have *a plan* to get on the property ladder as such – but dreaming of owning your own home has probably been on everybody's mind at some point!

PART 1

Chapter 1

Guarantor Mortgages

Guarantor Mortgages are probably the most widely-known method of helping someone get on the property ladder. A guarantor mortgage is where a parent or very close relative guarantees 100% of the debt. In other words, the guarantor agrees to cover the mortgage payments if the family member fails to do so.

The guarantor's income is then taken into account in addition to the borrower's and the potential mortgage size, and therefore potential purchase price, is increased. The number of lenders offering guarantor mortgages has been declining over the past 10 years, but they are currently available through a handful of lenders. If considering this route, there are a several factors that you will need to consider:

- Additional stamp duty. If you are named on the mortgage, then some (not all) lenders will insist that you are also named on the deeds of the property. If you already own property, this is likely to incur the additional stamp duty loading of 3%. Now, as I say, not all lenders will require you to be named on the deeds and actually 'Joint Borrower Sole Proprietor' mortgages have become more common over the last 18 months (as a direct result of the additional stamp duty charge coming into effect). So do check the requirements with both your lender and solicitor to determine the impact this will have on stamp duty.

- Maximum Age. Most banks and building societies will require a mortgage to be paid by the age of retirement. The actual age a bank uses as retirement age varies, but typical rules I see are 68, 70 and 75. Because your income is being calculated within the mortgage calculation, it is likely the lender will set the term based on the age of the eldest applicant; namely you. So a 65-year-old being named on a mortgage where the lender's maximum age is 75 will mean a maximum term of 9 years. Considering the typical and most affordable term for a mortgage is between 25 and 35 years, that means a term of 9 years will lead to unaffordable monthly payments. So, whilst a guarantor mortgage might increase potential borrowing, the monthly cost may make that mortgage size unviable anyway. Remember though that not all banks follow the same set of rules. Some have no maximum age and some base the age calculations on the highest earner not the eldest applicant. So don't assume this is a deal breaker until you have looked at all the lending options.

- Risk. You will need to look at a worst-case scenario and decide if you could fund the mortgage payments (potentially for a good few months) until your family member was able to resume making payments or the property could be sold. In an ideal world, you would not be named as guarantor for the whole mortgage term but instead would be removed from the mortgage when there was enough income for the main borrower to take on the mortgage in their sole name. If the property is held in joint names though, this removal is known as a transfer of equity and will incur legal costs but may also trigger stamp duty on the transfer.

- Credit Score. By being named on the mortgage, any issues with late payments will also have an immediate effect on your credit score, which may in turn affect your ability to obtain further credit in your own right. In some cases, having this financial link will mean you are also impacted should there be late payments or issues in other forms of credit held by the borrower.

Chapter 2

Helping with the Deposit

If guarantor mortgages are the most well-known method, then helping with the deposit is the most widely-used method for helping a family member when it comes to purchasing a home. It is often the case that people have sufficient income to borrow the amount they need, but managing to save the deposit in a timely fashion is the biggest challenge. As I'll cover in Part 2 of this book, the minimum deposit tends to be 5%.

Although 100% mortgages are available, these tend to come with very high interest rates or very restrictive criteria. It may also be the case though that they have the required minimum deposit, but by boosting their deposit you will be able to help them reduce their interest rate. Interest rates tend to improve with each additional 5% deposit you have. So rates with a 10% deposit are better than those with a 5%, but not as good as those with 15%. (NB. someone with a 13% would have access to the same rates as someone with a 10%. They would not see a potential rate improvement until they reach the next threshold of 15%.)

The main ways of helping deposit-wise are:

- A financial gift
- A loan
- Placing savings in a linked account
- Investing in the property with them

Financial Gift – Most banks will accept a deposit that has been gifted. It is likely they will require something in writing confirming that it is indeed a gift and you have no financial interest in the property. It is also likely that the bank and your solicitor will need to confirm your ID and source of funding, so don't be alarmed when you are asked to provide bank statements and passports. The beauty of a gift is not only that it might improve the interest rate, it also improves buying power. If a family member has a deposit of £30k and is able to get a mortgage of £200k, then that means their max price is £230k. However, with a gift from you, that would essentially be added on top of that £230k. So a gift here of, say, £50k boosts the potential property price to £280k. Apologies if that is stating the obvious, but you'd be surprised how many times I have to explain that.

A loan – If you have money sitting in a bank account, what interest rate are you earning? In 2019, the average interest in a simple savings account was 1.35% (compared to 11.8% in 1989!!!). The average interest rate for a loan of £5k is 8.04%. If you could lend money to a family member at a rate between these two numbers, then you are improving your returns and providing a lower interest rate to them. A win-win. Now, most banks will not be comfortable with a loan agreement such as this providing the deposit, however there are those that will. And any loan repayments will need to be taken into account when the bank assesses the family member's affordability. But I have seen many instances where providing the funds in this way works very well.

Placing savings in a linked account – Banks have been innovating mortgage products over the last few years as a direct result of seeing the help that 'Bank of Mum and Dad' is providing. One such product being used by a handful of banks allows borrowers to take out a mortgage for 100% of the property value. This is made possible where a parent or family member deposits 10% of the property value into a linked savings account. The money in those savings earns interest, but the savings cannot be accessed for three years. The idea behind this is that should there be difficulty in paying the mortgage or a situation of negative equity (where the mortgage balance exceeds the property/sale value) then these savings can be utilised by the lender. However, after three years, if all has gone smoothly, then the savings can be accessed/withdrawn by the parent or family member and invested elsewhere. At this point, one would hope that the property value has increased significantly, and a remortgage based on a 95% or 90%, or indeed 85%, loan to value can be achieved. The rates are higher than if you were to simply put down a 10% deposit, but the key here is the ability to have the funds returned after three years.

Investing in the property with them – As we discussed earlier, if your savings are not getting the returns you want, then why not consider property? Investing with a family member then alters from being a gift or loan and becomes more of a business proposition. For example, you provide 10% of the property value, and the homeowner buys the property with the plan that at some point in the next 10 or 15 years, for example, they can purchase that share back from you. The property would be revalued at the time of buy-back (by a RICS surveyor or alternatively an average of three estate agents' valuations) and they would simply pay you 10% of the new value. Thus, you will benefit from any increase in the property value. You could secure your interest in the property by placing a charge on the property or registering a deed of trust (I will discuss these in more detail in the legal considerations chapter). A point to note though is that some banks will not allow the deposit to be provided in this way where there will be an interest in the property. So you will need to check with the bank or your broker that this structure is acceptable.

Inheritance tax considerations – Children won't have to pay any immediate tax on any money gifted and parents/family members won't pay any tax on the gift either. However, further down the line, an inheritance tax bill could be due. There is a £3,000 per year exemption that everyone is allowed to give and it is immediately exempt from inheritance tax. And you can carry over any unused allowance from the previous year. In money terms, this means that two parents can gift up to £12,000 to a child if no gifts have been made in the previous year. If the gift is to be more than that though, then the money could be liable for inheritance tax.

If the person making the gift were to die within seven years, then it would still be classed as their estate for inheritance tax purposes. If the total estate, including the gift, is worth more than £325,000 (or £500,000 from 2020 onwards if part of estate is made up of residential property and is being passed to a direct descendant – residence nil rate band) then up to 40% tax would be due on the excess.

The amount of tax due decreases as the seven years go by:

Years between gift and death	IHT tax rate
Less than 3	40%
3	32%
4	24%
5	16%
6	8%
7 or more	0%

Whether the money is a loan or gift will also make a difference, so getting advice in this regard from a financial planner or a wills and trust specialist is definitely a good idea.

Chapter 3

How to Fund the Gift or Loan

When considering making a gift or loan, remember to consider your current financial circumstances and also your likely future expenditure and financial commitments. Consider whether you can afford to give the money. If the answer is "yes", then there are a number of sources that this money could come from. These sources might include:

- Savings held on deposit – Do remember though to ensure there is enough for yourself to cover emergencies, etc.
- Tax efficient savings – Tessa's, ISA's, LISA's etc. Cashing in tax-efficient investment, such as an ISA, will mean that you then lose that allowance. Ie. you cannot take the money out and simply put it back into that tax wrapper at a later date, as there will be limits on amounts that can be invested in any tax year.
- Cashing in pension – Only consider this if you do not need the potential income that a pension provides, and remember that the encashment may incur income tax which could eat into your money substantially.
- Investments such as bonds or stocks and shares – Again, be careful of any tax incurred from an encashment and that you may not be encashing at the right time (for example, when the fund value is lower due to a dip in the stock market.)
- Selling an asset such as a buy-to-let property – Whether any capital gains tax is due should be considered here.
- Taking out a mortgage or lifetime mortgage – A standard mortgage may not be possible due to age (most banks have a

maximum age of 75), but lifetime mortgages are specifically designed for the older generation who are unable to utilise standard mortgages. (In the next chapter, I will cover these in greater detail.)

However you intend to fund the gift or loan, you should ensure you don't need the funds yourself any time soon and that you both fully understand the terms of the gift/loan. To give you an idea about how others are finding funding, a report from Legal & General in 2019 confirmed:

In most cases (59%), the money is a gift with no requirement to pay it back, and a further 14% of borrowers receive a mix of a gift and loan. And only 6% of those who received financial help from friends or family were charged interest. Among those who are providing the help, just 8% say they have taken or would want an equity stake in return for their help. (https://www.legalandgeneral.com/bank-of-mum-and-dad/bomad-report-2019.pdf)

And, with most monies coming in the form of a gift, it is then also interesting to see how that gift was funded:

Over half (53%) of lenders say they drew or would draw on their cash savings to provide the money, while 21% took money from ISAs. This is often the result of deliberate planning. About one in five (19%) of those supporting purchases save money in a specific savings account; 13% use a Help-to-Buy or Lifetime ISA in their children's name to take advantage of the 25% bonus the government provides for first-time buyers; and about one in ten (9%) say they have invested in shares or other assets for the specific purpose of helping with a house purchase. Not all lenders have such nest eggs, however, which means they tend to draw on a range of sources — from cashing in their pensions as a lump sum (9%), using equity release (16%), downsizing (14%) or even taking out further borrowing themselves (6%).

The interesting thing to take from this is not only the statistics, but that funding to help people get on the property ladder is happening every day up and down the country, making it a key part of today's culture.

Chapter 4

Equity Release / Lifetime Mortgages

Equity release is a method of accessing the cash in your property. It can be done by taking out a mortgage secured on your home (lifetime mortgage) or selling a portion of your home to a provider (home reversion). You can do this if you are over 55 and you can either take the money as a lump sum or in smaller amounts over time (drawdowns) or a combination of the two. Considering that this is a potential option for raising funds to make a gift to a family member, it's certainly worth finding out about each option.

Lifetime Mortgage

You take out a mortgage secured on your property provided it is your main residence, while retaining ownership. You can choose to ring-fence some of the value of your property as an inheritance for your family. You can choose to make repayments or let the interest roll up. The loan amount and any accrued interest is paid back when you die or when you move into long-term care.

Interest rates must be fixed (or capped with an upper limit) for the life of the loan so there are no nasty surprises.

Lifetime mortgages are the most popular form of equity release, often using the option to roll up the interest so there are no monthly payments to make. However, if your concern is keeping the overall cost down, then there are products that allow you to make payments. The amount you can pay might be based on your income, so providers will have to check you can afford these payments. Assuming payments are maintained, then you should be able to maintain a legacy for your beneficiaries.

With some products, you can withdraw the equity in small amounts as and when you need it. This can be cheaper than taking a lump sum upfront, as you only pay interest on the amount you've withdrawn.

You retain ownership of the property, and, if it increases in value then you can still benefit from that.

Lifetime mortgages are generally available from the age of 55. You can normally borrow up to 60% of the value of your property, but exactly how much can be released is dependent on: your age, the value of your property, your health (some lenders offer larger sums to those with certain lifestyles, such as being a smoker, or health conditions, such as previous issues like a heart attack, stroke, etc), the amount of any outstanding mortgage or debt you have.

Some additional factors to consider:

- **Interest roll-up vs interest only** – You can choose to pay the interest if you have sufficient income which keeps the loan balance from increasing. Or you can choose to not make payments, and the interest will be added to the mortgage on a monthly basis. For each subsequent month, you are then paying interest on the initial loan plus interest on any interest already added. This means the debt will increase over time. The figures below illustrate how much the debt would be if you borrowed £50,000 at an interest rate of 3.55% on an interest-roll-up basis. (Source: Exchange Sourcing System.)
  - After 1 year   £51,804
  - After 5 years   £59,695
  - After 10 years   £71,271
  - After 15 years   £85,092

- **Lump sum vs income** – If you are borrowing to gift as a deposit, then it is likely you will be taking a lump sum. However, some lifetime mortgage providers allow you to take a drawdown. This means they will agree a reserve amount of funds that you can draw on at any time, subject to minimum withdrawal amount and other terms and conditions.
- **Cashback** – Some providers will provide a cashback in addition to any additional borrowing, which will not incur interest but may mean you are paying a higher rate due to the cashback.
- **Set-up costs** – The Money Advice service estimate set-up costs to be in the region of £1,500 to £3,000. The costs that you incur are likely to include:
    o Valuation and legal costs (although some providers will offer a free valuation).
    o Arrangement fees to the lender.
    o Arrangement fees to an adviser, such as a broker who specialises in equity release advice.
- **Redemption Penalties** – Many lifetime mortgage products come with complicated redemption penalties should you redeem the mortgage early. Redemption penalties often apply for a minimum period of 10 years.
- **Local Authority Benefits** – Some means-tested benefits can be affected by taking out a lifetime mortgage, so you should check if any benefits you currently receive might be affected.

Home Reversion

Home Reversion schemes – You sell your home, or a percentage of it, to a home reversion provider in return for a discounted lump sum or regular payments. You have the right to continue living in the property until you die, rent free, but you have to agree to maintain and insure it. You can ring-fence a percentage of your property for later use, possibly for inheritance. The percentage you retain will always remain the same regardless of the change in property values, unless you decide to take further cash releases, and you can benefit from increased house price on the percentage of the property you own. At the end of the plan, your property is sold and the proceeds shared according to the remaining proportions of ownership.

You will not get the full market value of your home. Rather than being charged interest by the provider, as with a lifetime mortgage, they are simply buying some or all of your home at a discount in exchange for letting you live there rent free until your eventual death or you go into care. The percentage of the market value you will receive depends on how long the provider thinks you will continue to live there – so the older you are when you take out the plan, the more they are likely to pay you, although it can still vary from one provider to another. These schemes tend to release more capital from the property than is possible through a lifetime mortgage. Most plans are available from the age of 60 or 65.

Home reversion plans are often considered to be high-risk products and you should consider carefully if they are right for you. The reason they are considered high risk is that you sell a portion of your home at a substantial discount. If you died a short while after selling this portion, then the value of your estate will have been dramatically reduced, perhaps unnecessarily.

Some things to consider:

- **Set-up costs.** Similar to a lifetime mortgage.
- **Local authority benefits.** Similar to a lifetime mortgage.

In addition to a lifetime mortgage and a home reversion scheme, you could also consider a 'retirement interest-only mortgage'. This works in a very similar way to a traditional interest mortgage except that:

1. The loan is usually only paid off when you die, move into long-term care or sell the house.
2. You only have to prove you can afford the monthly interest repayments.

The banks would look in detail at your income and expenditure and decide if your income was sufficient to make the interest payments. There are similar considerations with that of lifetime and home reversion, so you should seek advice as to the suitability of this.

Chapter 5

Discounted Family Purchase/Gifting Property

If you currently own a property, such as an investment property or second home, and you no longer wish to retain it, then gifting the whole or part of the property might be an option. You could gift the whole property or simply gift the deposit.

Gifting the deposit

Some banks allow buyers to take advantage of something known as a discounted family purchase. This is where you sell the property to a family member at a discount to its value and that discount is classed as the deposit from the bank's perspective. This means that the buyer doesn't have to provide any deposit at all (but will still need money for costs such as stamp duty). As an example:

Property Value	£300,000
Agreed price to family member	£270,000
Banks assumed loan to value (LTV)	90%

So the family member would organise a purchase mortgage of £270,000, but costs and stamp duty would be payable on the £300,000 figure.

Only a handful of banks allow the deposit to be funded in this way, so speak to your bank or broker to see if this option is available to you.

You should also investigate tax treatment of this transaction from both a capital gains tax and inheritance tax perspective.

Gifting the whole property

If you wish to, you can of course simply gift the entire property to your family member. However, the property will need to be mortgage free at the time of gift and, again, you should investigate the impact this would have on tax for yourself.

Chapter 6

Other Considerations

Within a property purchase there are various legal considerations that need to be taken into account. This not only applies to someone buying a property, but also I think it is important to consider legal implications for anyone looking to help a buyer – whichever method that help takes. I thought the best way to cover any legal issues would be to speak to a lawyer to cover some of the key questions that I often get asked. Fiona Lumsden is an expert real estate solicitor and Head of Legal Services at Nested. Before joining Nested in 2019, she was at the London law firm, Healys LLP. She specialises in residential property transactions.

Question 1: 'If there is a parent or grandparent looking to make a gift, when should that gift be transferred and who should it be transferred to?'

The gift can either be transferred prior to the donee finding a property or during the conveyancing process; it is really up to the donor when they want to transfer the gift to the donee. Crucially, it should be made prior to exchange of contracts in any event to ensure the donee will have all of the funds in place for completion in order to commit to exchange of contracts.

The donee's solicitor will require evidence of the funds transfer from the donor to donee (so certified bank statements) and confirmation of the source of funds and identity of the donor (certified ID and AML – Anti Money Laundering – checks will be undertaken). They will also request a signed 'letter of gift' from the donor confirming the sum transferred and that they have no further interest in the sum given and will require no repayment in the future; a donee's mortgage lender may require sight of this also.

Question 2: 'If I have gifted some money to my child and they go off and buy this property with their partner, is there any way of protecting that gift in the future in terms of if they split up and sell the property and then their ex-partner gets my money that I gifted?'

Once a gift is made, it is usually not protected as gifts don't tend to have any obligations or conditions attached to them. A parent that wishes to gift their child a sum of money to purchase a property may ask their child to protect the gift if the child is purchasing in joint names with a partner or friends, or the child may already believe this necessary to do so in any event. If so, the donor should think about executing a Declaration of Trust.

A Declaration of Trust is a legally-binding document between the donee and their partner to expressly set out what will happen to the portion of funds that were gifted should they end their relationship after purchasing the property and have to sell or transfer it. So if the parent gifted their child £50k towards the purchase price, and the child put in all of the £50k and their partner put in only £10k, the Declaration of Trust may state they each receive those respective amounts on future re-sale or transfer of the property and all other profit or loss is shared, or even distributed, in accordance with those initial percentage proportions. The gift is therefore protected.

The Declaration of Trust can be held directly by the signatories or registered at the Land Registry on completion of your purchase. It is better to have it registered as it may be misplaced or destroyed accidently otherwise, and will be difficult to prove it existed.

It is important to note, that should the donee marry the partner in the future, the Declaration of Trust would be considered by the

Court in any divorce proceedings. It would be good evidence to confirm the intention of the parties at the time of the purchase of the property, but may still not be agreed by the Court. It is therefore important to obtain legal advice from a family solicitor on such matters prior to going into a property relationship with a partner, usually where large sums of money are involved, to ensure you understand from the outset how any funds may be distributed in the future as your relationship with your property partner changes.

It is also worth noting that should you fail to sign a Declaration of Trust when you purchase the property and have to sell the property later on due to a relationship break-up, if the split of funds cannot be amicably agreed, you will need to ask the Court to decide how the funds should be distributed. It is therefore very important to keep a record of any sums contributed so you can prove the same.

Further info on this point is also covered in the Wills section.

Question 3: 'If someone is giving a loan as opposed to a gift, what recourse does that person loaning the money have if, for example, they need their money back or the interest payments are not being made?'

A loan is different to a gift as it will be clear from the outset that the amount is repayable at a later stage. The terms of the loan would be agreed upfront – for example, how and when interest is payable or the events in which the loan is to be repaid, such as on default of interest payments. Having the terms recorded in a loan agreement will help avoid any confusion in the future as to what was agreed.

A loan that is not recorded by way of a written legal agreement is not protected, as the intention of the parties at the time the funds were given cannot be expressly known – you would need to prove the funds were given as a loan and not a gift. If the loan was agreed in writing, it would also be less protected if not registered as a charge against the property. A charge is a legal document signed by the borrower and which is registered *against a property* at the Land Registry so as to alert any potential buyer of the existence of the debt. It is therefore always prudent when providing a loan to have the terms agreed in writing and registered against the property at the Land Registry. On sale of the property, a purchaser's solicitor would ensure all charges registered against the property are to be repaid on completion of the sale.

If you provide a loan and need your money back, without an event of repayment noted in the loan agreement being triggered, then you can only ask for repayment and hope for the best. You cannot demand repayment unless the terms of the loan expressly state that the loan could be called back at any time. If however, there is a default of the terms agreed, such as late or no-interest payments made, subject to certain minimum criteria, you can request the Court to make an order for repayment of the amount owing. So recourse for repayment of a loan is always better and easier if the terms are agreed in writing and registered against the property.

A lot of banks are less comfortable with a loan as a deposit, as opposed to a gift, but there are some that are okay with it under certain terms. Gifts are therefore the most popular way of advancing funds to your children for a property purchase to assist with getting on the property ladder, as they are more acceptable to the majority of mortgage lenders; they have less of an impact on affordability as no repayment or interest is applied to the sums given.

Question 4: 'If a parent or grandparent is helping the son or daughter onto the property ladder with some money, can they be named on the property?'

You can have up to four named individuals on any property title recorded at the Land Registry.

On a cash purchase, should a parent or grandparent wish to be named on the property title, this would be fine as long as this is agreed by all parties. Whereas, on a purchase with mortgage finance, it is uncommon for mortgage lenders to allow a parent or grandparent who has provided funds to be named on the property title also, unless they were named on the mortgage documents too.

If you are a first-time buyer, it may also be less beneficial to purchase a property with your parent or grandparent noted on the title, as they will likely already own property and this may impact the amount of stamp duty payable on completion. So there are tax implications to consider when agreeing who will be named on the property title. You should therefore obtain advice from a tax specialist prior to purchasing in order to structure the purchase as best as possible to suit yours and, if applicable, also your mortgage lender's requirements.

Chapter 7

Wills

Wills become very important to consider when gifting or loaning monies. As with the legal questions, the best way to cover these points is to speak to a specialist Wills and Trust Estate Planner. Victoria Lykke-Dahn, Estate Planning Associate at Radcliffe & Newlands Estate Planning (RNEP), with over 20 years' experience has the following advice:

If making a gift, then that gift will be absolute and there is no recourse to the funds in the future. However, you may want to consider protecting it in the future so that your gift doesn't end up in the hands of an ex-partner, for example.

This protection could be achieved by creating a trust whereby the money is put into the trust and then the trust gives the family member the money. The upside of the trust is that it is a gift and will therefore qualify for inheritance tax relief. (Ie. If you live for at least 7 years after the gift, then it is removed out of your estate for inheritance tax purposes, saving your family money in the long run.) If making a loan, then the monies will not fall outside of your estate for inheritance tax purposes. Also, another point to note is that you would need to ensure the mortgage lender for the purchase is ok with any trust arrangement and, as such, do mention the trust to the mortgage broker.

Victoria and her team can be reached on:
enquiries@rnestateplanning.com, Tel: 0207 3820446.

Remember to visit my website
www.scottrawlings.co.uk for lots of additional
resources and information as well as links to my
Getting on the Property Ladder podcasts.

PART 2

Chapter 8

How Much Can I Borrow?

This is the question that I get asked the most. Nine times out of ten, people want to know the maximum they can borrow – and there is nothing wrong with asking that, because you want to know your limit so that you can make sure that you work within it.

Up until a few years back, this was a pretty easy question to answer relatively accurately. You could look at someone's income and if they applied a multiple of 4 to 5 times that amount, it would give a pretty accurate figure of how much you were going to be able to borrow when you eventually spoke to the banks. You would then be able to take that figure and off you would go and start to look at properties, etc. It was pretty straightforward and if there were two people buying, you would simply add their salaries together and multiply it by 4 or 5 times and that would end up giving you the figures you needed.

Then, a few years back, there was some additional regulation that came into force as part of the Mortgage Market Review (MMR). This was really the regulator saying to the banks, "Look, we're not very happy with the way you're lending money at the moment. We want you to do a few more checks and be more cautious when it comes to working out how much someone can borrow."

When the banks are looking at how much someone can borrow, yes they want to know what the salary is. Then they look at things like extra income: overtime, bonuses, commission. Each of the banks does something different here. But if you looked at a typical rule, they will want to see a track history (with some banks it's 12 months' track history and with others it's two years). But if there is a track history, they may take into account up to 100% of that income. Now, not all banks are going to do that. Some will only take 50%, some will take none of it, some might take a quarter. They all look at it slightly differently, but actually if there is a two-year track history, then some will take all of that into account. That is then the additional income they are going to look at.

Then, they are going to drill down a layer of detail and they are going to look at what you're spending on things like debts (ie. loans, credit cards, student loans, car finance, hire purchase, interest-free credit.) All your debts, basically, and they are going to look at the expenditure on that. Then, they are going to drill down another layer. They are going to look at regular expenditure. This is things like pensions, child care costs, travel costs, gym membership, fixed amounts of money that come out of your account each and every month.

And then, they are actually going to go a stage further and they are going to look at three months' worth of bank statements. This is almost to the point of "How much do you spend on coffee each day?" and "How much do you spend at the weekend?" They are going to do some proper analysis, not just on monies you've got coming in, but also on what you've got going out. All the banks have got weird and wonderful affordability calculators now, so they would put all that data in and that will then spit out a number which is how much they are going to lend. For an accurate figure of how much someone can borrow, you should go and speak to your mortgage broker or speak direct to a bank, and they can plug your information into their affordability calculators to give you that figure. I definitely recommend you do this. But, I want to give you a figure to take away today.

So the net effect of all these extra checks that they're doing is that the amount they're lending now is coming in at around 4.5 times income. So, if you want a pretty safe figure to start analysing how much you might be able to borrow, using a multiple of 4.5 times will give you a fairly good idea. But use that as your starting point, because actually some banks will only lend three-and-a-half times, some might lend more than that – maybe 5 times, maybe even five-and-a-half or even 6 times. Use the 4.5 times figure as a rough guide, but it's very important to get that verified.

If you are self-employed, it depends on how your income is structured. If you are a limited company, then the lender might look at salary and dividends or they might look at salary and profit; if you're a sole trader, they might be looking at net profit. Again, each lender has a slightly different way they look at self-employed income, but the typical rule here is that they will take an average of the last two years' income and then they will take that income and add that to the employed person's salary, for example, and then give it the multiple of 4.5. The only time that is slightly different is if the most recent years' figures are lower than the previous years. If that is the case, you might find that they will only take the most recent year, they will not take an average because they might think it is a declining trend.

And while we are on the subject of the self-employed, it's a myth that lenders don't like self-employed people. It's just that a lot of self-employed people have great accountants, which means that they might pay less tax than an employed person due to the various allowances they can offset, but it does however therefore mean on paper that their income isn't as high as might be needed to get the mortgage amounts that they feel they can afford. But lenders are totally happy to lend to self-employed people. Some banks do require that someone has been self-employed for at least three years. Some will be happy with two years and actually a select few will also consider lending with a 12-month trading history.

That is the first part of the puzzle: how much can you borrow. We now need to look at what sort of deposit you need to be aiming for.

> Visit my website www.scottrawlings.co.uk for links to my podcasts – you will hear interviews with first-time buyers and find out how much of an income multiple they ended up borrowing.

Chapter 9

Size of Deposit

How much of a deposit you are going to need has actually changed a lot over the years. Traditionally, when it came to the deposit, you would either have been putting down no deposit at all, so getting a 100% mortgage, or 5%, 10%, 15%, 20% or 25%. The general rule of thumb here is that the bigger the deposit, the better the interest rate you are going to get.

But, you've got to be hitting those thresholds to access the different rates. So, in other words, someone putting in a 6% deposit is going to get the exact same set of rates as someone putting in a 5% deposit. You don't open the up the new rates until you hit that next threshold, which is the 10% deposit. The bigger the deposit, the better the interest rate tends to get.

In 2008, the UK went through a period commonly known as the credit crunch. This was a period when the UK economy shrunk, house prices fell, banking debts were written off and lending became harder to obtain. The credit crunch led to a disappearance of 0% deposit mortgages and it also got rid of 5% deposit mortgages. So, for a long time, the minimum deposit anybody needed was 10%. Then, the government introduced the help-to-buy scheme (which I'm going to talk about a bit later on) and that brought back 5% deposit mortgages and actually there are now lenders that have once again started lending at 100%. Therefore, 'technically speaking', you do not need a deposit to be able to go out and buy a property. However, those 100% mortgages have much higher interest rates and they are actually much more difficult to qualify for.

On the subject of 100% mortgages, as I mentioned in Part 1, there are a few banks that have introduced some fairly innovative products in that space. The way they work is that the client can borrow a 100% of the property value, so they don't need to find a deposit. However, a parent or family member has to deposit 10% of that property price into a savings account with that same bank. That 10% sits there in that savings account earning interest, however, the parent or family member cannot access that money for three years.

The idea behind this is that the bank has a pot of money to fall back on should there be a situation of negative equity or the mortgage not being paid. After those three years though, the deposit money can be taken out and spent by the parents, and then the client is left with a mortgage on the property. Hopefully, by this stage, the property value will have gone up, so when they come to remortgage they will no longer be at 100%, they will maybe be at 95% or 90%, and might be able to improve on the interest rates. So, 'technically speaking', you do not need a deposit to buy a property. However, it is harder to get a mortgage without a deposit, so if you're going to take a figure away from this I suggest you aim for a minimum 5% deposit.

Another point to mention here is that the bigger the purchase price, the bigger the deposit you may end up needing. This is because lenders do not like taking too much risk once the property values get more than around £500,000 or £750,000. So, at those levels, you might not be okay with a 5% deposit, and you might need to be hitting a 10% and even a 15% deposit.

I have mentioned that rates improve as the deposit level increases. Rates are still competitive now if you compare them to five or ten years ago. With a 5% deposit, they are just not as competitive as with a 10% deposit. And those are not as competitive as with a 15% deposit. But this is where it is always good to speak to a broker or your bank and just see how the rates change at those different levels. Because if you were at 9%, and by finding an extra 1% deposit your rate improves dramatically, then if that saves you a lot of money over the long run, it might be worth considering.

Chapter 10

Upfront Costs

On top of your deposit, you're going to need a chunk of money for all the different costs involved in buying a property. The costs will depend on the purchase price. In a moment, I will go through an example, but before I do that I will run through all those costs and explain what they are.

First of all, you have stamp duty. Stamp duty is the government tax that applies every single time you buy a property. The amount you pay on stamp duty is dependent on the purchase price of the property. Now, to work that out, you can go on the HMRC website. They have calculators on there, but I'll just talk you through the numbers as this can be quite useful to know.

There are some special rules with stamp duty, so what I'm going to do first is explain the standard rules and then I will run through what the special rules are.

You pay no stamp duty on anything between 0 and £125,000, so if you're lucky enough to buy for less than £125,000, there is no stamp duty. You then pay 2% on the next £125,000 (so, between £125,000 and £250,000). You then pay 5% on the next £675,000 (so, between £250,000 and £925,000). You then pay 10% on the next £575,000 (so, between £925,000 and 1.5 million). You then pay 12% on anything above that.

Special rules to do with stamp duty

If you are a first-time buyer, and the definition here of a first-time buyer is that you've never owned a property, anywhere in the world, ever. You can't have owned one year ago, you can't still be named on a property abroad – you've literally never had your name on the deeds of a property. If that is the case, and you are buying for £500,000 or less, then you actually pay no stamp duty on the first £300,000.

So let's say, for example, you are buying a property for £350,000, and you are a first-time buyer, you would only be paying stamp duty on sums between £300,000 and £350,000, which is 5%. So, it's 5% of £50,000 which is £2,500.

So, that's a great rule introduced by the government because it can save you up to £5,000. But, you've got to be a first-time buyer, and if there are two people buying, you have both got to be first-time buyers and you've got to be buying for £500,000 or less. If you're buying for £550,000, unlucky, you still have to pay that normal stamp duty that we worked out.

The second special rule that I want to mention to do with stamp duty applies to anybody buying a second home, or anybody buying a buy-to-let property where they already own a property. It's basically at the point where someone owns multiple properties, and they will pay the stamp duty that I've just detailed and then, on top of this, they are going to pay an additional 3%. Now, this rule came in on 1 April, 2016, and the reason this rule is interesting for first-time buyers is that this has put a lot of investors off buying a property.

Putting people off buying a buy-to-let property could be a good thing for first-time buyers, as it means there are less people competing for properties that they are trying to buy. They are not suddenly up against loads of investors who are trying to buy the same properties that they want to buy.

The other reason it is potentially relevant for first-time buyers is that there is also something called 'let to buy'. This is where someone owns a property already that they live in and they want to move house, but they don't want to sell that property. So what they do is rent out that property and then go off and find a new property to live in. For those people, even though they are keeping their old property, and the new property is for them to live in, they still have to pay that extra 3% as well.

The reason this is relevant to first-time buyers is that this rule has put off a lot of home owners from doing this. They may have intended to rent out their property originally, but as a result of this 3% rule coming in, they changed their minds and thought, "Do you know what, instead I'm going to sell because I don't want to pay that extra 3%." So this could be a good thing for first-time buyers because it is likely to mean there are more properties coming on the market than there would have been before.

So stamp duty is the biggest cost; all the other costs are a lot less than that.

Next, you have solicitor's costs. A solicitor's job is to do the legal work involved when you are buying a property. They will look at the land registry, they will look at the title deeds – if it is a flat you are buying, they will go through the lease and check there are no conditions that are problematic. They will also do things like contact the council, make sure there is no planning permission for a motorway outside your property, make sure it is not built on a mine – they are going to check all the legal aspects of this purchase.

Solicitors are so key to the whole process, that you definitely, definitely want to make sure that you have a good one.

The solicitor can be anywhere. They don't have to be local to the property; they don't necessarily have to be local to you. The most important thing is that you take a recommendation. We have seen lots of clients where the biggest stress comes in the legal side of things, so getting a recommendation for a solicitor who is very good is a really great idea. Cost wise, I would budget for between £1,500 and £2,000, depending on the purchase price.

Next up, you need a survey on the property and there are three types of survey you can have done: basic, homebuyers and full structural.

Basic is purely done for the bank. It doesn't really tell you anything about the condition of the property. Even though it is done for the bank, you pay for it and I'd say the costs for this depend on the price of the property, but something in the region of £400. I should emphasise again though, that this does not tell you anything about the condition of the property.

If you want to know a little more about the property, you can go to the next level which is the homebuyer's report, which will give you a 10- or 15-page report on the general condition. This includes comments on aspects such as whether there is damp or comments on the electrics. It uses a traffic light system where green means something is totally fine, yellow means it might need attention and red means it's pretty serious and you really need to get this looked at straight away. So it's a general commentary about the property and it's about a 15-page report. The cost for this is probably nearer £600. If you have a homebuyer's report, you don't need to have the other one as well – so it's £400 or £600.

Next up is the full structural survey or the building survey. This is the most detailed report where a building surveyor will go in and conduct a full on check of the property. They will go into the roof space, they will look at the condition of the walls, they will look at everything. This gives you more detail, so is therefore more expensive. The cost for this is probably nearer £800, but you have to have the basic as well so it's £800 plus £400.

Here is a little tip for you. If you get the bank to do their basic report and have the really detailed report at the same time, it will save you about £100, which can seem tempting. However, don't ever do that. You do not want the bank doing a full survey and knowing everything about the property. This is because banks are cautious at the best of times and the more they know about the property, the less likely they are to want to lend against it or they might hold money back, (this is called a retention). Or they might insist on specialist reports. You want to know everything about that property, but let the bank do the minimum survey they need, the valuation, and then and organise a more detailed report off your own back.

The type of survey you have done depends on what you are buying. So, if the property is a brand new house or flat, for example, it will probably have a 10-year guarantee: two years of any defects, eight years of major defects. So therefore, in that situation, you'll probably be okay with a basic report. However, if it is an older property and you are spending a lot of money on it, it might be worth considering getting it checked out because those surveys can also be quite useful bargaining tools. If that structural survey comes back and says that the roof needs work, for example, then you can go back and negotiate on the price or get the vendor to do the work. So it can be a really useful thing to do, but it often depends on the type of property that you are actually buying.

Next, you have lender's fees. Most banks will charge you a fee for the pleasure of borrowing money from them. They all call it something different – booking fee, completion fee or arrangement fee – but generally speaking, there is usually a fee somewhere in the world of mortgages. A typical fee is between £500 and £1,000. This can be added to the mortgage, so it doesn't necessarily come out of your saving pot, but if you do add it then you will be paying interest, which over a 25-year period might be quite a lot. Ideally, you want to get a good balance of low interest rate and low set-up fee. Some mortgages come without a set-up fee, but then they tend to have higher rates than those that do, so you need do a bit of maths and look at whether it is worth paying that fee or not to get the better rate. It's therefore good practice to budget for some sort of fee as part of this process.

The only other costs you need are moving costs – a man with a van or whatever you choose.

Example: Potential Savings Required

£350,000 Purchase price for a first-time buyer	
Stamp Duty	£2,500
Solicitor's fee	£1,750
Survey – Basic	£400
Homebuyer's	£600
Full Structural	£800 plus £400
Lender's Fees	£1000
Deposit (Min 5%)	£17,500
TOTAL	£23,350 (assuming homebuyer's survey)

(These costs are designed to be an estimate and accurate figures should be obtained from the solicitor and bank or mortgage broker).

You therefore need your pot of money for a deposit, *plus* these extra costs. If you go to a bank or mortgage broker and say, "Right, I've got a 10% deposit, but I haven't got any money for the costs," from their perspective, you haven't got a 10% deposit because they know that some of that money has to go towards stamp duty, etc. Therefore, you have probably only got an 8% deposit and, as a result, you will be within those rate brackets. Therefore, when you are looking at how much you need to save and how much you need to put by, you want to be aiming for the deposit plus all these costs.

Some of these costs are not needed until further down the line. Stamp duty, for example, is not payable until completion, which is when you get the keys. On average, that can take up to about three months, so you do still have time to save up for these costs – but you need to know that you will definitely have that money when you need it, because otherwise you will not be able to complete on your purchase which would not be acceptable at all.

Chapter 11

Monthly Costs

The next piece of the puzzle is how much this mortgage is actually going to cost you per month. The monthly payment on a mortgage totally depends on how you structure it. There are lots of variables which we'll come to a bit later on, but it's useful to have some sort of idea of what these costs are likely to be. A very rough way of working out mortgage costs is if you use the following calculations.

This is a calculation to work out how much a 25-year repayment mortgage on a fairly average interest rate costs. What you do is take the number of thousands you are going to borrow, multiply that by 5, and this gives you the monthly payment. In other words, if it was a £100,000 mortgage, you would calculate 100 x 5 = 500 – so a £100,000 mortgage would cost around about £500 a month. A £200,000 mortgage costs around about £1,000 a month, and so on.

This is a very rough guide to give you a ballpark figure of what mortgage costs are likely to be, but the true monthly payment on the mortgage will vary. For example, you might not pay it back over 25 years, you might instead choose to do it over 35 years. You might get a really good rate because you have a large deposit, which might bring down that cost too. But you can use this calculation as a rough way of working it out, and then it's a good idea to speak to a bank or broker just to see how much your mortgage payments are likely to be based on current rates and your personal circumstances.

There are other costs that you need to budget for on top of the mortgage. First of all, if you are buying a flat, you are likely to have ground rent and service charge. You don't pay this when you rent a flat, but you do when you own a flat. Now, if that is a house that has been split into two flats, the service charge might be £20 a month. However, if that is a big block of flats, with lifts and concierge and similar services, you might be looking at nearer £300 a month. So it's very important to ask the agent, "How much is the ground rent and service charge?" because you are going to need to budget for that.

Then you will need to set money aside for various insurances. There is buildings and contents insurance – this is where you are insuring the property itself and what's in it. Then, there are policies such as: life insurance, critical illness cover, income protection (this is where you are insuring yourself).

It is a good idea to look at the different insurances and work out, either with an advisor or with your bank, which insurances are most appropriate to you, looking at what your work provides, what you need separately and what you can use your work benefits for.

Budgeting an amount per month for insurances is good practice. I would suggest somewhere between £50 to £100 is a fairly good idea. The next chapter will cover some of the considerations around insurances.

All of the other costs are pretty much what you would end up paying when you are renting. For example, council tax, utility bills, etc. So doing a budget planner is a really good idea – factoring in your mortgage costs, plus these additional costs, and just checking that it will still be affordable.

You can find a free budget planner online at my website www.scottrawlings.co.uk as well as links to my podcast where we discuss how much your mortgage will cost as a percentage of take-home pay.

Chapter 12

Insurances

The terms 'life insurance' and 'life assurance' are often interchangeable and both often known simply as 'life cover'. People often ask what the difference is, so here's how it works:

Life insurance is cover you take out for a set number of years. You agree the term of the policy at the outset, usually between 10 and 25 years. This is why you'll often find this type of policy referred to as term insurance.

Most people tailor their policy to ensure that their financial commitments would be met in the event of their death, so policies are often aligned with the term of a mortgage or other loan. Banks and building societies usually require some form of life insurance as a condition of granting a mortgage.

Parents often opt for life insurance to cover them while their children are growing up, taking a policy that will end when their offspring become financially independent. With life insurance, you aren't guaranteed to receive a payout as you could outlive the term of the policy. However, what you do get is the continuing peace of mind and the guarantees that protection policies give you and your family.

Life assurance, by contrast, is designed to provide cover until you pass away. It can be more expensive than life insurance as it covers you for a longer term and pays a lump sum in the event of death, whenever that occurs (subject to premiums being maintained). You may have heard the phrase 'whole life' or 'whole of life' used in relation to this type of policy.

Other types of cover that provide valuable protection:

When people think about protection insurance, they typically think about a traditional life policy that can protect for a specified number of years or for a whole lifetime, and pays out a lump sum on the death of the policyholder. But nowadays there are many other types of policy that can also have a major part to play in protecting and providing for the financial needs of you and your family.

Mortgage Payment Protection

What it does – Mortgage payment protection policies are designed to cover the cost of your mortgage payments if you're sick, have an accident, or become unemployed and can't work.

How it works – Generally, the policy will start paying out either 31 or 60 days after you are unable to work. Most policies will pay out for a maximum of one year.

What you need to know – With statutory sick pay set at just £85.85 and only payable for up to 28 weeks, many families would struggle to meet their mortgage payments if disaster were to strike. The amount payable under the policy is usually around £1,500 to £2,000. So, if you have a large mortgage, you will need to consider how you would cover any shortfall.

You can choose the date at which the policy would pay out in the event of a claim. This can range from a month to up to a year.

Policies that pay out sooner will have higher premiums.

Income Protection

What it does – This type of policy pays a monthly income tax-free if you are unable to work due to an illness or injury.

How it works – The monthly income under the policy will be between 50 and 70 per cent of your salary and will be paid until you are fit enough to return to work or reach retirement age.

What you need to know – State benefits aren't generous and only a few employers will continue to support their staff through a long illness, so income protection policies can help families through difficult financial times.

You can choose the date at which the policy would pay out in the event of a claim. This can range from a month up to a year.

Policies that pay out sooner will have higher premiums.

Critical Illness

What it does – Critical illness cover pays out a tax-free lump sum if you are diagnosed with a major illness, including cancer and heart disease. Actual illnesses covered in a policy may vary between providers.

How it works – Many insurers will make a part payment on an early-stage diagnosis of a condition specified in the policy; the percentage will vary from company to company.

What you need to know – Many people buy a combined life and critical illness policy, and it makes sense to do so. In this case, a payment would be made on either diagnosis of a critical illness as defined in the policy, or death, whichever is the sooner. If the cover is combined in this way, the policy premium is usually cheaper than it would be for separate policies, as there is only ever one lump sum paid out by the insurance company.

Family Income Benefit

What it does – Family income benefit policies work in a similar way to ordinary life cover, but instead of a lump sum, the policy pays out a regular income if you die.

How it works – A typical policy might be taken out by the parents of young children, so that if one parent were to die during the term of the policy, then an income would be paid out for a predetermined period of time. So, if you had a 20-year policy and were to die five years into it, then the policy would pay out a regular income for the remaining 15 years.

What you need to know – Family income benefit insurance is a simple way to provide your family with an on-going income rather than a lump sum if you were to die. Critical illness can also be added that would provide a pay-out if either parent were to be diagnosed with a serious illness.

Accident, Sickness and Unemployment

What it does – This policy provides cover so that if you are unable to work because you're injured or sick, or through no fault of your own, you have lost your job.

How it works – In the event of a claim, you will receive a predetermined percentage of your monthly income, usually for a period of up to 12 months. Payments are made after a waiting period of at least a month. If you choose a longer waiting period, your premiums are likely to be lower.

What you need to know – Accident, sickness and unemployment cover differs from mortgage payment protection which is designed specifically to cover your repayments on a specific debt such as your mortgage. It differs from income protection insurance in that it includes unemployment cover.

Private Medical Insurance

What it does – Private medical insurance means that you can get access to diagnosis and treatment faster and therefore are more likely to recover quicker. Policies cover the costs of private medical care including seeing consultants and specialists, treatment, surgery, private hospital accommodation and nursing costs.

How it works – You will need to decide what level of cover you want for yourself and your family, as this will determine what your premiums will cost. You can choose the level of excess, that's the amount of any claim you are happy to pay yourself. Paying a higher excess will generally bring the cost of premiums down.

What you need to know – There are conditions which insurers won't pay out for, including cosmetic surgery and alcohol or drug-related illnesses. You may find illnesses that you've suffered from in the past are excluded from cover as they are deemed to be 'pre-existing conditions'.

And finally don't forget Buildings and Contents insurance.

Home & Contents Cover

Home insurance is vital to protect the roof over your head and all your possessions. It's simple to arrange, and acts like a shock-absorber, protecting thousands of families each year from the financial effects of life's unwelcome events like burglary, loss, fire and flood.

Choosing from the hundreds of policies on offer can be bewildering and time-consuming. That's where using an adviser can be of real help in finding you the best and most suitable deal for your needs.

Buildings Insurance

This type of policy covers the bricks and mortar and permanent fixtures of your home. So, if it's damaged as a result of events like storms and floods, fire, vandalism or water damage from leaking pipes, your policy will cover the cost of repairs to your property.

The amount of buildings insurance you need should represent the cost to rebuild your home, not its full market value which can often be a lot higher. Your adviser will

be able to help you calculate the right level of cover for a property of your type, size and construction.

You will generally need to have buildings insurance in place under the terms of your mortgage loan, and you will be required to include the name of your insurer on the policy schedule.

Contents Insurance

Contents insurance policies are designed to cover your possessions from loss, damage or theft.

Insurers define 'contents' as all those things that you'd take with you if you moved house. So, most policies include things like furniture, carpets, curtains, electrical goods, clothes and valuables such as watches and jewellery.

The cover available falls into two types: 'new for old' policies which means that, if for instance, something is stolen then the pay-out will be enough to buy an equivalent new item. Indemnity policies, which are often cheaper, pay out a reduced amount

if you make a claim as they take into account the wear and tear or the depreciation in the value of an item. So, if you lost something you'd owned for a while, you would get back the current value, not what it would cost to buy new.

The amount of cover you'll need, referred to as the 'sum assured', needs to be adequate for your needs so that you don't risk being underinsured. Being underinsured would mean that your insurer might restrict the amount they would pay out in the event of a claim.

Simply walking around your home with a notebook and pen can help you compile a comprehensive list of what you own. Don't forget to include those things you store away in cupboards, basements and attics too.

Valuable items away from home – You can get cover for belongings you have with you when you're away from home. When taking out a policy, you'll be asked if you require insurance for various items such as mobile phones, laptops, jewellery and cameras. There is usually a limit on the value of any one item, and you may need to specify the items you want to insure.

Cover for additional risks – For further peace of mind, many people opt to pay for additional cover under their policy. You can, for instance, add insurance for legal expenses, home emergencies, drains and plumbing, freezer breakdown, accidental damage to home contents and accidental damage for personal possessions away from home.

Chapter 13

Different Mortgage Options

Interest Rate Type

The first thing you need to look at is the type of interest rate that is going to be most suitable for you.

The most common type of interest that people choose these days is a fixed rate. A fixed rate is a really good idea in a situation of uncertainty around interest rates or if someone is particularly cautious when it comes to money. A fixed rate is fixed at a set rate for a period of time – typically, for two, three, five or even ten years. If rates go up it doesn't matter; if rates go down, it doesn't matter. Your rate is fixed and therefore your monthly payment is fixed. At the end of that fixed rate, it then flips onto what is called the lender's variable rate, which is a floating rate. At that point, you're then free to renegotiate either a new rate with your current lender (depending on the bank) or you can remortgage to a new lender. In the same way that people swap credit cards around, that also happens with mortgages. However, it doesn't happen quite as often – maybe once a year, or after two to five years.

You then have a tracker rate. The tracker rate is linked to the Bank of England base rate, which means: if rates go up so does your rate, if rates go down then so does your rate. You can have a term tracker, which means it follows that base rate at a premium for the duration of the mortgage, so there is no jump to the variable rate. Or you can have a two-, three-, four- or five-year tracker which means that it does follow the base rate for that period of time, but at the end of that period it then flips onto the lender's variable rate in the same way that a fixed does, and you would need to renegotiate it at that point. The advantage of a two-year tracker is that it is generally cheaper than a term tracker; the downside is that you are having to renegotiate it every couple of years. A tracker rate is obviously useful if rates are going down. It's also beneficial if you're not cautious with money and you can handle the risk of movements in the interest rates and your monthly costs.

You then have a discounted rate. This is a rate that runs at a discount to the lender's standard variable rate. Lenders' standard variable rates are generally set by the lender at a premium to the base rate: they loosely follow what happens to the base rate, but they don't necessarily have to. At the moment, you can have a variety of lenders' variable rates ranging from 3.5% up to about 6%. A discount mortgage, also known as a discounted variable rate, has an interest rate that is set a certain amount below the lender's standard variable rate (SVR). It goes up and down when the SVR moves. Then, at the end of that two-year discount (if a two-year discounted rate), it flips onto the lender's variable rate in much the same way.

Term of Rate

Once you know the sort of rate that you want to go for, you then need to decide how long you want that rate for. So, if you're looking at a fixed rate as I mentioned, rates are fixed for two, three, five or ten years on average. There are different advantages and disadvantages with each of them. For example, a two-year rate is generally lower than a five-year rate, which means your costs per month are less. The other advantage here is that you then have the flexibility to renegotiate things in a couple of years' time – whether you might be moving house, looking to borrow more money, or hopefully getting a better loan-to-value because the property has gone up in that time, and therefore you can improve the rate. This gives you that flexibility.

The downside is that you are going to get whatever rates are around in two years' time. This means that if they have gone up over that two-year period, you might find your payments jump after two years.

With a five-year rate, you don't have that issue. You can literally forget about it for five years, but the downside is that it is generally higher than, say, a two-year; it's also not very flexible in that period of time. So if you wanted to change mortgage in that period of time, you might have a penalty. Penalties can be anything from 3% to 5% of the mortgage balance which can be quite a lot of money.

So you want to look at the type of rate that you are going for and the term of that rate based on your thoughts on interest rates but, more importantly, whether you need flexibility or not, whether you're likely to move, and whether you are fairly confident that you're not going to need to change the mortgage for that period of time.

Repayment vs Interest Only

You then need to decide on the mortgage type. There are two ways you can pay off a mortgage: repayment and interest only.

Repayment is where each month your monthly payment is made up of an element of capital and an element of interest. With each payment, the balance on the mortgage decreases and the proportion of capital versus interest also alters. In the first year of a repayment mortgage, a typical monthly payment might consist of 95% interest and 5% capital, whereas in the final year it will be more like 95% capital and 5% interest.

With interest-only, your monthly payment only consists of interest. People would typically then save money into an investment vehicle with a view to building up a lump sum to be able to clear the mortgage in, say, 25 years time. If the investment did well, then the mortgage could be paid off early or there would be a surplus. If it didn't perform well, then there would be a shortfall or the term would need to be extended. Endowments were typically used in the past, but these had a bad press due to poor performance and have been replaced these days with ISA's or other investments. Some interest-only providers, for example, don't require there to be an investment in place and instead are happy with the mortgage being repaid via, say, downsizing in 25 years' time. Interest-only mortgages however are very difficult to come by these days, so you will need to see if you fit the criteria if this is an option you wish to consider.

Repayment Mortgage

The diagram below shows how the balance of a mortgage reduces each year, if taking a repayment mortgage. The speed at which the balance reduces increases as you move through the term.

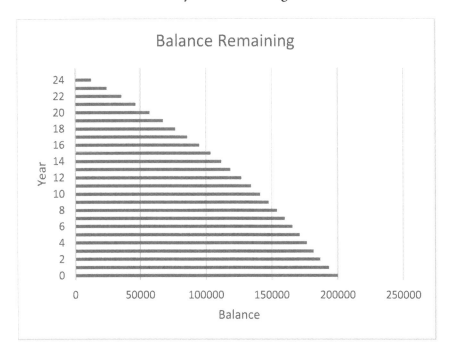

Mortgage Term

You then need to decide on the mortgage term. The most common mortgage term is 25 years, but that is simply because that is a figure that provides an often affordable monthly payment. However, the term you choose can be lower or higher than this. The general rule is that a mortgage needs to be paid off by the time you retire. Many banks assume that to be age 70. So this means a 35-year-old could take out a 34-year mortgage. A 50-year-old might only be able to take out a 19-year mortgage. The advantage of a longer mortgage term is that the monthly cost is less. However, the downside is that the interest payable over a 35-year term, compared to a 25-year term, is huge. Also, some lenders do allow the term to go beyond age 70, for example, if you can show sufficient retirement income to be able to afford the payments beyond retirement age. But do check with your bank or broker on the specific rules.

Chapter 14

Credit Scoring and Searching

The first thing a bank is going to do when they are looking at lending to you is either a credit check or a credit score.

A credit check is an underwriter looking at your credit report, whereas a credit score is a computer system that gives you points for various parts of your financial life. These are factors such as:

- Are you on the electoral roll?
- How long have you had a bank account?
- Do you have a credit card?
- How long have you been in your job?
- How many addresses have you had in the last three years?

At the end of this check, a computer will either say "yes" or "no".

Factors that will make it say "no" are things like: not being on the electoral roll, not having your bank statements sent to the same address that you are on for the electoral roll, (lots of people get bank statements sent to their parents' address, for example, but try to have the two married up.) Also, make sure that the way that your address is written on the electoral roll, is the same as the way it is written on your bank account, because something like a comma in one address and not the other means that they cannot marry it up electronically and this can then affect your credit score.

Additional negatives that work against you include: missing payments for bills, defaults, and county court judgements. All these things go against you on a credit score.

The first thing that you want to do is get your own credit report. There are lots of places that you can do this. Experian and Equifax are often the ones that the banks use, but there are lots of others such as: ClearScore, Callcredit and Credit Karma. Most of them will let you get that credit report for free. When you get the report, what you will really want to look at is whether there is anything on there that a lender might not like, such as a missed payment or you have applied for credit which has been declined. You also want to look out for inconsistencies such as how your name is written by each institution, and also how your address is written, and how it appears on the voters' roll for example. Some of those reference agencies will give you a score. That score is really just a useful guide, but it's not that relevant in the real world because each bank will have their own scoring system. In other words, you might get a great score at Experian, and then you go to a bank and fail because their scoring system is completely different. So, Step 1 is to check your credit report.

When you are closer to buying a property – and by this I mean you are actually doing viewings on properties and thinking of going back for second viewings – at that time, it is a good idea to get what is called a 'mortgage in principle' or a 'mortgage promise' or a 'decision in principle'. This is where a bank will do a credit check on you and confirm whether you have passed the score and they will give you a piece of paper that confirms that you can get a mortgage. Some of them will actually say how much you can actually borrow on that 'decision in principle' as well. It can be useful because you can then show the agent that you are able to get a mortgage and that your finances are all sorted. It is not 100% necessary, and it's often not worth the paper it is written on, because although someone has a piece of paper saying that they can get a mortgage because they passed the credit score, they might not actually be able to borrow against that property. This might be because the lender does not like that property or when the lender sees their payslips they may not like some of the deductions – so these factors might affect things. It is therefore useful to do this, but only nearer the time of purchasing a property.

Chapter 15

Estate Agents

Before we start talking about estate agents, I want to ensure that you are doing your research in all the right places. A good place to do your first bit of research is on the online property portals – the main ones being Rightmove, Zoopla and OnTheMarket. You should try and use all three because they have often got slightly different properties within them.

Another really good website to look at is Nethouseprices.com. The reason for this is that it will tell you sold prices in the area, which can be quite useful, but also once you have identified a street you like, it will tell you whether there are currently any other properties for sale in that area and, interestingly, whether or not they have recently changed their price. So you can see if property prices are going up or down in that area, which will also reveal whether there are people who are keen to sell who are therefore lowering their prices. So, this is an extra tool to use.

Having said this about the online tools, the best way to buy a property is to deal direct with an estate agent, because often properties get sold before they have even hit Rightmove or Zoopla.

Do your initial research online and once you have found agents in your area who are getting properties that are within your price bracket, then you want to contact those agents almost every week, asking, 'What have you got for me this week? What have you got for me this week?' You want to be the first person they think of when they take on a new property, and the best way of doing that is just to be at the front of their mind's eye.

Whatever they tell you, do your own due diligence. So, if they say that a flat is opposite a beautiful park, then go back to that park at night and see if indeed it is beautiful or if it is completely scary. Check everything that they say! Go back to the property at different times of day, try your commute at 8am and see how many trains you have to wait for before you can get on the carriage. Check all these things out. Look at the parking. Definitely, definitely take a viewing guide, which you can find at www.scottrawlings.co.uk.

But agents are key. The online agents are totally fine and there is no good or bad, you just have to deal with whichever agents are taking on the properties. But always remember to do your own due diligence.

While talking about agents, I thought it might be useful to get some insider tips from an agent. Hannah Betteley at Nested has some great tips to share:

Before And During The Viewing

The negotiation process starts from the moment you first make contact with the estate agent selling the property! Whilst it's easy to think that the agent is an intermediary who is simply working to achieve a sale, in reality, the agent works for the vendor and any good agent will do their utmost to achieve the highest possible sales price for their instruction.

Because of that, it's often impossible to get an agent who is completely 'on-side'. But all agents are human. And an agent that likes you is far more likely to try and get a deal agreed in your favour than one who doesn't! There is absolutely no harm in being courteous, punctual and friendly at all times.

Dos:

√ Arrive for the viewings on time.

√ Always give feedback and respond to calls/emails in good time.

Don'ts:

χ Don't make it obvious that you've fallen in love with the property.

χ Don't discuss your assets/financial situation in revealing detail.

What you should be asking the estate agent:

If it's a flat:

- How much is the service charge and ground rent? These are important if you're buying a flat. Ground rent, in particular, can affect mortgageability. Any property that has a doubling or proportional increase clause attached to the ground rent could be unmortgageable and should be avoided.

- Beware of any ground rent higher than £250/year, and any service charge higher than £2,500/year – ask yourself, what are you getting for that?

- How long is left on the lease? A lease length less than 81 years will limit your ability to get a mortgage.

- Who is the freeholder?

For all properties:

- What is the vendor's situation? Have they found an onward purchase? How flexible are they on price? A good agent acting in the best interests of their client won't give too much away here. But any information that you can glean will be useful in framing your approach to an offer, should you wish to make one.

- Is it a listed building? Is it in a conservation area? If the answer is 'yes' to either of these questions, then it might be more difficult to alter the property.
- How many viewings/offers has the property had? If the property has been under offer previously, why did it fall through?
- How much is the council tax?
- What is their view on the price? Does the agent think that it's realistic? If so, which recent comparables can they show you to substantiate it?

There will undoubtedly be some questions that the agent can't answer. Do ask them to check any unanswered questions with the vendor and follow up with you by email after the viewing.

Things to check for on the viewing

While offers made on properties in England are not legally binding, it's advisable to perform certain basic checks before committing time and money to engaging with the process of conveyancing.

Some things to look out for:

1. **Damp** (appearance or smell of). Are there any areas of condensation, peeling wallpaper, stains or discolouration?
2. **Basic structural damage** – eg. are there any cracks in the walls or loose roofing tiles? A survey will pick up things further down the line, but it's good to spot concerns as early as possible.
3. **Plumbing** – test the hot water pressure, and also several of the taps/toilet to make sure they work.
4. **Electrics** – check that there are enough electrical sockets for

your needs. Period properties that have not been recently updated can often have too few plug sockets for modern needs.

5. **Boiler** – how old is the boiler? And has it been recently serviced?
6. **Neighbours** – can the agent give you any information on who the neighbours are? Are they council tenants?
7. **Amount of natural light** (or lack thereof).
8. **Local environment** – check for nearby building works, eyesores or brownfield sites.

The market in relation to your approach

The wider London property market has seen sale volumes collapse as a result of Brexit.

Fewer transactions have for the majority of areas meant that prices are depressed, with both fewer buyers and sellers.

With the wider market assessment in mind, it is important to reflect the level of greater uncertainty in the amount that you are prepared to offer. Unless homes are very competitively priced, we are not in an environment where estate agents will be expecting multiple asking-price offers on properties, particularly if the property has been listed for a long period of time. On average, homes in London are currently achieving 91% of their initial asking price, which is a reflection of the fact that we are well and truly in a 'buyer's market'. It's important to use this to your advantage when negotiating and ensure that the agent is aware of your strong command of local market dynamics.

Agents will almost always talk up the level of interest in a property to stimulate a sense of urgency and bring forward offers. In some cases, what they are telling you about interest levels will be true, but in others it's merely a sales tactic – so be warned! Negotiations will always be determined in part by the vendor's situation. Knowing why you're prepared to offer what are you are will give you greater confidence in the purchase and more authority in the negotiation.

When Making An Offer On A Property – Three Things To Do:

1. Position yourself as the best buyer. Buyers in a strong position have the best chance of getting what they want.
2. Present your offer in the best light (see example of offer letter).
3. Know your limits. This can be difficult, particularly when you find the home of your dreams.

1. Positioning Yourself As A Buyer

(i) Being proceedable

To ensure that the acting estate agent and the vendor take you seriously, it's important to have several things lined up before submitting an offer.

- If you first need to sell a property in order to buy, has your sale exchanged contracts? Buyers in the strongest position are those who have certainty over the sale of their own property and are in a position to move quickly.
- If you haven't exchanged on the sale of your property, is it on the market and under offer? Being in a 'chain' is quite common, but it doesn't put you in a particularly strong bargaining position given the current rate of fall-throughs in London (circa. 44% for 2018).
- Failing that, some vendors will sometimes entertain offers from buyers who are not yet under offer, but are on the market and actively trying to sell. The acceptance of such an offer will likely only come if the vendor is in no particular

rush to sell or if the buyer agrees to additional terms, such as paying full asking-price and offering a non-refundable deposit. Even so, it is unlikely that any agent would advise them to stop entertaining viewings if under offer from a non-proceedable buyer.

(ii) Have your finance in place

Many estate agents will ask to see proof of funds before submitting an offer to a vendor, and most will request to see confirmation of a mortgage agreement in principle or speak to your mortgage broker to ensure that you are able to proceed with a purchase.

- Getting a decision in principle can be quite a quick process, but it's essential to understanding your budget, as well as how much you can negotiate.

(iii) Instruct a solicitor

You can instruct a conveyancing solicitor to act for you on the purchase of a property free of charge. You should always aim to do so before submitting an offer so that should your offer be accepted, you can move quickly and get terms of sale into your solicitor's hands and begin the conveyancing process.

When instructing a solicitor, it is important to go on recommendation. The conveyancing process is known to be particularly slow when conducted ineffectively and can easily result in a deal falling through if badly handled.

2. Presenting your offer

When it comes to the offer itself, there are several schools of thought regarding what is best practice, and what is most effective in securing an agreed price.

There is a trend for people to offer a very *precise* number and claim it to be their best and only offer, aiming to show that they have calculated the absolute maximum they can pay for a given property. From my experience, that technique is unlikely to engender the best result. In a strong sellers' market, first and best offers are often advisable, particularly when there offers being made by multiple parties. However, that's certainly not the market that we're in at the moment. In a buyers' market, the buyer holds the power and has the scope to test the water with an initial low offer.

It's important to not act desperate and if your first offer is rejected, take your time when increasing your offer, or even ask for a counter offer from the vendor. I would suggest a maximum of two offers and with the second offer make clear that it will be your final offer, after which you will be taking your business elsewhere.

Here is an example of what you should include in an offer email:

Subject: 135b Ashmore Road – offer in writing

Hi Alex

Thanks again for taking the time to show me around the property.

I would like to submit a formal offer of £530,000 for the leasehold of flat 135B Ashmore Road. I propose a targeted exchange date of +3 weeks from the receipt of a full contract pack, and completion a month thereafter or at a date that is suitable to the vendor.

If the vendor wishes to move quickly, we can carry out private searches to expedite the process, as well as bring forward the completion date.

Conditions of an accepted offer:

    i.   The property is removed from your website and all of the portals. I would ask that the property remain so, provided that reasonable progress is being made on the conveyancing.

ii.   *I would also ask that memorandums of sale are sent out before the end of the week, so that my solicitor can begin the searches.*

The funds will be a mixture of cash and borrowings. I have a mortgage in principle arranged with Nationwide at an LTV of 60%. Please see below for the details of my broker should you wish to confirm. I will send proof of funds for the remainder of the money in a separate email.

Below you will also see the details of my solicitor, who has been instructed and I have attached a copy of my ID as well as proof of address that is dated within the last 3 months.

Whilst this is the only property I am offering on, I would greatly appreciate it If the vendor could get back to me as soon as possible because I have several other viewings lined up for next week and would like to secure something very soon.

If there is anything else that you require, please do let me know.

Best wishes,
John Smith

Solicitor details:
Tel:
E:

Mortgage Broker details:
Tel:
E:

3. Know your limits

It doesn't matter if you've found your dream home and it really is one in a million! The estate agent works for the vendor, and you don't want them to think that they can squeeze every last penny out of you because you've fallen madly in love with the property in question.

It's important to make clear that the property you are offering on is your first choice, and that you do not *currently* have any other offers out on the table. You do however want the agent, and therefore the vendor, to think that you have options elsewhere were your offer not to be accepted.

Assess each property and determine how much it is worth to you and set a ceiling on the amount you are willing to pay. If your offer is not accepted, don't immediately rush back with an increased offer. Rather, sit back and tell the agent that the offer will stand for one week, after which you will restart your search.

Estate agents will often try to pressure buyers into making an offer by telling them about competing interest. Of course, in some instances this can be true, but in others it's simply a sales tactic. If there is other interest, ask the agent, "Are they proceedable buyers?" and try to determine what their position is in relation to your own. If by 'interest' they mean interest from people who can't proceed with a purchase, then you know that the pressure isn't on quite yet.

Gazumping and How to Avoid It Happening to You

Whilst the practice of gazumping has declined in line with market confidence in the run-up to Brexit, it still happens and can prove to be an annoyance and an expense if solicitors have been engaged. You might expect this controversial practice to be illegal, but it's not. Under English law, the agreement between you and the seller does not become legally binding until contracts have been exchanged.

The government is looking to bring in measures to reduce the number of buyers who fall foul of the practice by introducing what are known as voluntary reservation agreements. However it's safe to say that their introduction is still some time away. There are several things that we recommend doing in the meantime to minimise the chance of it happening:

1. **Get the property taken off the market.** This means removing it not just from the agent's website, but also getting it removed from Rightmove and Zoopla. Some agents will mark a property as 'Under offer' but this is still dangerous for anyone who has that property under offer – ie you. Estate agents must report all offers by law, so it's important to try and minimise the number of people who see the home subsequent to it going under offer.

2. **Insist on an exclusivity agreement.** This is an agreement between you, the seller and the estate agent not to entertain offers from other buyers for a set period of time. Vendors will likely insist that certain conditions are met on an agreed timeline, such as mortgage and structural surveys being booked in or a non-refundable deposit being paid. Anything that shows a cash commitment to the purchase can be enough to justify the agreement. These agreements can be drawn up by solicitors, but it will add expense and time to the sale. A lot of people will agree to a verbal agreement, though this will not come with the same level of protection.

3. **Take out home buyers' protection insurance.** This is very much optional and will not decrease the likelihood of a fall-through from happening. It typically costs around £50 and will cover you from the expenses accrued in the run up to exchange such as survey cost, conveyancing fees and mortgage lender fees. You can find out more about it on the Home Owners' Alliance website.

4. **Finally, befriend the seller!** It's a simple tip, but it can be very effective in ensuring that they think twice before entertaining another offer.

There are a number of free tools online that will give you help on other factors that can assist with the decision-making process. One Dome – https://www.onedome.com/locality-reality/explore – provides a useful area assessment search which can tell you all about local parks, schools and restaurants, amongst other things, for most London areas.

Local schools can also factor heavily in the decision-making process and are worth being

aware of, particularly regarding the resale value of a family home. Locating –https://www.locrating.com/schoolsmap.aspx – will give you a good overview of the schools in the area, and in slightly more detail than the Rightmove and Zoopla tools.

Similarly, the government's school comparison website – https://www.compare-school-performance.service.gov.uk/find-a-school-in-england – gives a comprehensive breakdown of schools at all levels, searchable by postcode.

Local crime statistics can also factor into decision making and the Metropolitan Police

Neighbourhood search – https://www.police.uk/metropolitan/ – can give you a breakdown of the local area's statistics.

If you are interested in air quality, Airview – https://airview.blueair.com/ – provides a really useful search service.

Remember to visit www.scottrawlings.co.uk for downloadable versions of the offer letters and also tips and stories from first-time buyers about dealing with agents on my podcast.

Chapter 16

Are Some Properties Harder To Arrange Mortgages On Than Others?

There are certain property types and situations that are harder to get mortgages on than others. I will just give you a couple of quick examples.

First of all, anything that has Japanese knotweed in the garden. Japanese knotweed is a weed that effectively can knock a house down. Ok, maybe that sounds a bit dramatic, but it can definitely damage your property and cost you thousands to rectify the damage. It takes something like three years' worth of chemicals to get rid of. It is a total nightmare! Often found on gardens that back onto railway lines (because the railway companies used to plant it to give their banks and sidings stability) which up and down the country is a lot of gardens. It is not impossible to get a mortgage, but if knotweed exists it is your surveyor's job to point that out and it needs to be undergoing a treatment by specialists to get rid of it. It just means less banks will lend on the property. Some won't lend where knotweed exists at all.

If you are buying a flat above a shop, it depends on what that shop is, but that can make the mortgage a bit trickier. This applies especially if the shop is selling anything hot and smelly like fast food, which can be difficult. Again, this is not impossible, there is just less choice of banks.

Ex-council properties tend to be okay, but once this gets more than five floors high then this is where it can become difficult.

So a good thing to do, if you are not sure about a property, is to get in touch with your bank or broker and ask, "Am I going to be able to get a mortgage on this?" They will be able to go and speak to their surveyors before you've even started spending money on a survey.

A couple of other issues to watch out for are concrete construction and deck access. There are various types of concrete construction. It depends on the exact type, as some lenders are okay with it and some are not. The reason they are less keen to lend is that certain pre-fabricated concrete has been known to have structural issues. It also has less saleability, as there is less demand for these properties than, say, a traditional brick-built terrace.

'Deck access' is another issue to be aware of. This is where you are walking along a balcony past another person's front door (or doors) to get to your own front door. Again, it is not impossible to get a mortgage, but you may find that there is less choice of banks.

If you've got any stories around unusual properties, then get in touch at www.scottrawlings.co.uk – I'd love to hear about the weirdest properties you've come across!

Chapter 17

Help To Buy

Help To Buy is the government scheme that has been introduced to help people get on the property ladder. There used to be two schemes, but now there is only one. The one that currently exists is the help-to-buy equity scheme. This is the one that is for new-build properties only.

The way this works is that when you put down a 5% deposit, the government will give you a 20% equity loan, so they will give you 20% towards that property. You will then go and get a mortgage for the remaining 75%. If you are buying in one of the thirty-three Boroughs of London, you can get up to 40% from the government. So 5% deposit, 40% government and 55% mortgage.

That 20% or 40% that the government gives you is interest-free for five years, but after five years you start paying interest on that as well as the amount you are paying on the mortgage.

It is a good scheme because it boosts your buying power. A bank might say that your budget is £300,000, but by using that extra money from the government then you might be able to buy for £400,000. If that gets you into an area that you want to live in, it might be worth considering. Albeit you won't own the whole property yourself.

That 20% or 40% that the government is giving you means that they own 20% or 40% of your property, which means that if you sell it in two years or ten years or fifteen years, they will get 20% or 40% of whatever the property sells for. So if it goes massively up in value, they will see their money increase.

There used to be another scheme that was part of the Help To Buy. That one was for older properties as well as new-build. With that scheme though, there was no government assistance to the buyer, it was effectively 5% deposit and a 95% mortgage. What happened was that the banks starting lending 95% anyway, so there wasn't any need for the scheme. As a result, the scheme has gone, but it doesn't matter because the banks will lend 95% anyway.

Saving for a deposit

While we are on the subject of Help To Buy, a good place to save your deposit is in the help-to-buy ISA or the Lifetime ISA. The reason that it is a good place to save your deposit is because you get interest on your savings, and then when you come to buy, the government will have boosted your savings by up to 25%. There are a lot of rules around this and I shall now summarise the key points.

How a Lifetime ISA works

If you're buying a home with someone else you can both take advantage of separate Lifetime ISAs.

- You can save a maximum of £4,000 into a Lifetime ISA each tax year.
- The Government pays a 25% bonus on the savings, which is paid monthly.
- The maximum government bonus each year is £1,000.
- The amount you pay into the Lifetime ISA forms part of your total annual ISA allowance (£20,000 for 2019/20). Eg. if you pay £4,000 into your Lifetime ISA, you can still pay £16,000 into other ISAs.

- Other types of ISA include: cash ISAs, also stocks and shares ISAs.
- You can pay into a Lifetime ISA until you are 50, which means if you saved £4k per year from the age of 18, you could earn just under £32,000 in bonuses from the government in that time.

Who can get a Lifetime ISA?

To be eligible for a Lifetime ISA, you must be:

- Between the ages of 18 and 39.
- A UK resident, or a member of the armed forces serving overseas, or their spouse/civil partner.

Using the ISA to buy your first home

You must be a first-time buyer to put the Lifetime ISA towards your first home. A first-time buyer is someone who does not own, and has never owned, a home anywhere in the UK or the rest of the world.

To be able to be eligible for the government bonus, you must have opened a Lifetime ISA at least 12 months ago.

The home you buy must:

- be in the UK
- have a price of £450,000 or less
- be the only home you will own
- be where you intend to live
- be purchased with a mortgage.

If you're buying with someone else and they are also a first-time buyer, you can put both bonuses towards the purchase of your home. The price of the home still must not be more than £450,000.

If you're buying a home with someone who has owned a property before, they don't count as a first-time buyer. But you can still put your own bonus towards the price of the home you're buying together.

You can use your Lifetime ISA with other government schemes as long as you meet the eligibility requirements of the other schemes you wish to participate in.

You can use the Lifetime ISA to buy land for a self-build property as long as the purchase meets all the other criteria for property purchase through the scheme.

Taking the money out of your Lifetime ISA

There are three scenarios whereby you can access the funds built up in the ISA and without tax:

- You reach the age of 60.
- You are diagnosed with a terminal illness.
- You're buying your first home and your account has been open for 12 months.

You pay a withdrawal charge if you take the money out for any reason other than those three reasons. The charge is 25% of the amount withdrawn. Therefore, only really consider using a Lifetime ISA if the funds will definitely be used for buying your first home or to save for retirement.

Savings Calculators

There's lots of useful information online which can help guide how much you need to save as a deposit. There are lots of useful calculators online. Let's say, for example, you were looking to save up £20,000 over the next three years. Assuming your savings were earning interest of 2%, then by saving £500 per month you would have saved £20,000 after three years and three months. The interest rate you earn will have an impact on how much you need to save, and for how long, so it's definitely a good idea to shop around for the best savings account interest rates.

Shared Ownership

Another scheme to factor in is Shared Ownership. Again, Shared Ownership is a useful way of buying a property if you can't afford to buy in an area or the type of property that you want to live in. Let's say that your budget was £200,000, but all the properties in your area were £300,000. With shared ownership, you can buy a share of that £300,000 property. Let's say you bought a 50% share: you would put a deposit down and get a mortgage on £150,000, then you would be paying rent for the other half. It's just you that lives there, but you are paying mortgage and rent each month so it can be expensive, but it's helped a lot of people across the country get on the property ladder. In the future, you can buy bigger shares and that's called 'staircasing' which means the property is revalued and then you pay the percentage of that new value as and when you want to do it. Again, this is a good scheme that has helped a lot of people, but with this scheme there are lots of rules. These include: rules on how much you can earn; rules on where you can buy based on where you currently live; etc. But it is certainly worth considering.

Other Considerations:

Solicitors (The legal stuff)

Most people know a lawyer/conveyancer is needed during the house-buying process, but most people don't know what they do. Fiona Lumsden is an expert real estate solicitor and Head of Legal Services at Nested. Before joining Nested in 2019, she was at London law firm Healys LLP. She specialises in residential property transactions. Here are her responses to some of the most common legal questions I get asked.

Question 1: 'What does a solicitor do in the process?'

Most importantly, your solicitor makes sure you can obtain legal title to the property on completion of sale and that you will have no issues on resale of the property in the future. Your solicitor is also there to listen to you; they will want to know why you are purchasing the property, your immediate and future plans, and any works that you may want to complete. They will take this into account when investigating the legal title to the property, and the information provided by the seller so they can make sure there is nothing that could obstruct those plans.

For example, if you want to complete a rear extension or loft conversion, they will ensure there are no restrictions and advise you of any planning and building regulations information you should be aware of. Similarly, if you want to purchase the property as a buy-to-let, or wish to let it out in the future, they will check there are no restrictions on underletting. You should therefore make your solicitor aware of any plans you have for the property, and this is especially important if you are purchasing a leasehold property, as there will be more restrictions on what you can and cannot do with the property during your ownership.

Lastly, if purchasing with a mortgage, they will ensure that your mortgage lender's requirements are adhered to. This is very important, as once you have exchanged contracts you are legally bound to purchase the property and will forfeit your deposit funds if for any reason you cannot complete the purchase. Confirming your mortgage lender's requirements have been met, so that funds are in place and ready to be released to you, is therefore crucial.

So, your solicitor is there in the home-buying process to make sure the property can be registered in your name on completion of sale and ensure you can sell it again in the future, understand your plans for the property and advise you of anything that could affect or change these and, if purchasing with a mortgage, confirm that your mortgage funds will be released on time to complete your purchase. By looking out for you and your interests, your solicitor should make the home-buying process as easy and stress-free as possible, which in turn should enable you to be less worried about the process and more excited to purchase your new home.

Question 2: 'There are loads of solicitors out there – how should someone choose a solicitor and do they need to be a solicitor or a conveyancer?'

Understanding the meaning of "conveyancing" is important to distinguish between a solicitor and a conveyancer – conveyancing is essentially the transfer of property from a seller to a buyer. So, whilst a solicitor has the ability to specialise in many different areas of law (such as conveyancing, employment, family or tax law), a conveyancer can only specialise in conveyancing (i.e. property matters).

So, a solicitor specialising in conveyancing (a conveyancing solicitor) will be an expert in conveyancing, just like a conveyancer. They are both regulated by different bodies; a solicitor is regulated under the Solicitor Regulation Authority (SRA), whilst a conveyancer is regulated under the Council for Licenced Conveyancers (CRC). Although they are regulated by different bodies, they will both work in the same way (the home buying process and their duties to you remain the same) and they are both held to the same service level standards and requisite expertise for completing the conveyancing work on your behalf. Whether you use a solicitor or conveyancer, it's reassuring to know that both will be regulated and fully insured to complete your purchase.

So, choosing between a solicitor or conveyancer doesn't matter necessarily. What you should look out for in making your choice is how experienced they are; a solicitor may not be as experienced as a conveyancer and vice versa. What really matters is that you get a sense of their experience, credentials and capability. It is also important to ensure you get on well and will enjoy working with each other, as a typical conveyancing transaction can on average take around six to ten weeks, during which time you will have numerous telephone and email conversations. Making sure you understand from the outset how they work and what service you can expect, what their working hours are, and whether they have a dedicated assistant or secretary or shared support team, means you know who to contact during the conveyancing and how best to get in touch for both general or urgent matters.

It is always helpful to get referrals from family friends, your estate agent or mortgage broker. Your family or friends may have purchased a property already and will have engaged the services of a solicitor or conveyancer previously – they can tell you how impressed they were; whether there were any areas of service they would have liked a bit more help on; and any tips on getting the most out of the person they referred to you.

This will put you at an advantage as you can trust the referral and rely on the pointers given to you, giving you the opportunity to be transparent with your solicitor or conveyancer from the outset as to what you expect and want to achieve. Setting these parameters from the beginning means you and your solicitor are aligned and have the same information, which can be beneficial for a speedy, stress-free purchase. You can normally get a referral from your estate agent or mortgage broker as they will have worked on numerous property sales previously.

Question 3: "If someone is looking at buying a leasehold flat are there any things that you feel, from a legal perspective, they should be aware of or consider?"

When buying a leasehold flat, it is important to understand that whilst you will own the flat (there are some leasehold houses also) and become the 'leaseholder', the 'freeholder' (also known as the landlord) will own the building the flat is within (or for leasehold houses, the land, estate or development the house is on) and will require you to comply with the terms of the lease granted. The lease is thus the set of rules and regulations, rights and restrictions, which the leaseholder promises to abide by during their ownership of the flat. It also confirms the layout and extent of the property that the leaseholder owns.

From a legal perspective, anyone looking to buy a leasehold flat should ensure there are no terms in the lease that may affect the way in which they intend to live and enjoy the property during their ownership or that could affect a future purchaser's ability to live and enjoy the flat when it comes to resale of the flat in the future. For example, whilst you may not be purchasing the flat as a buy-to-let investment property, a future purchaser may want to do so, and any restriction preventing the letting of the property may affect the saleability of the property at that point. So it is crucial to know what the general requirements and plans for your flat are, and what a future purchaser may require, and to make sure there are no restrictions that may prevent this.

There are a number of core legal areas to look out for when buying a leasehold flat, such as:

- an acceptable remaining lease term for you and your mortgage lender,
- adequate rights of access to the flat,
- necessary rights of use and support from the structure of the building,
- any restrictions or onerous provisions relating to the use of the flat or ability to alter the layout or extend the flat,
- acceptable level of ground rent and ground rent review provisions,
- reasonable level of service charge and confirmation of any planned increases in the next couple of years,
- confirmation of the services provided by the freeholder for the building generally,
- any past, present and future planned major works to the building,
- standard building insurance arrangements,
- any past or present complaints about the flat or the neighbouring flats or their owners,
- that the lease plan matches the floor plan of the property as seen on your property visit.

If there are any prohibitive or onerous provisions, or the lease plan is inaccurate, now is the time to ask the freeholder via your solicitor or conveyancer whether they can be amended. This is done by way of a document called a lease Deed of Variation – this may be problematic and costly, and will likely delay your purchase, but will be worth it in the long run and will also prevent any issue on re-sale of your flat.

If any amendments cannot be agreed, you should carefully consider whether the flat still suits your needs and requirements before committing to exchange contracts; this is the point at which you will be legally bound to buy the flat. Now is also the time to ask your solicitor or conveyancer of any provisions in the lease which you don't understand and to also confirm that you understand what your rights and obligations are during your ownership of the flat.

Making sure the level of ground rent, and the ground rent review provisions are within acceptable parameters for you and your mortgage lender, is very important. This will not only have an affect on your affordability now, but also later on, should your lease have a ground rent review provision for increasing ground rent – it could also affect the saleability of your flat, depending on what another buyer considers to be an acceptable level on future re-sale of the flat. Your solicitor or conveyancer will be able to advise you on what current acceptable levels of ground rent and ground rent review provisions are for each mortgage lender. At present, mortgage lenders will require any ground rent review to increase in line with the Retail Price Index (so not doubling or increasing as a percentage of the value of the flats in the building), reviewed not more frequently than every 25 years and to remain within £1,000 per annum in London, and £250 per annum outside of London, during the term of the lease.

Question 4: What is the implication if someone were to withdraw from a purchase after exchange of contracts has actually happened? I know it is rare but what are the actual implications?'

This is very rare because you should be aware of all of the information relating to the property prior to exchange of contracts and have confirmed that the property suits your needs and requirements. You should also already be aware that exchanging contracts legally binds you to purchase the property and that the consequences of withdrawing are very costly.

However, should you need to withdraw from a purchase, the most first and most notable consequence is the forfeiture of your deposit funds. If you paid the usual 10% of the purchase price, this would be forfeited and the seller would be entitled to retain the same. If you paid less than 10%, there is usually a term in the sale contract, noting that the full 10% is immediately payable to the seller should you withdraw from the purchase following exchange of contracts, so you would be required to immediately make up the balance deposit funds and transfer the same to the seller.

Secondly, you would be liable to the seller (and likely to the other parties in the chain that have suffered a financial loss as a result of you withdrawing) for any out-of-pocket expenses they have incurred. This could mean any mortgage application costs, survey costs, legal fees, hotel costs, removal charges, and any other costs or charges that would not have been incurred but for you withdrawing from the purchase following exchange of contracts.

Should you not have the funds for the full amounts owing you may be summoned to Court and a Charge placed on any property you already own for the full outstanding amount. If you do not own any other property, an attachment to your future earnings could be agreed by the Court so that the amount owing will be paid over the course of time as a deduction from your employment earnings.

Question 5: 'When exactly in the process do you need to give the solicitor money?'

This is a question that I frequently get asked. Buyers want to know when payments need to be made so they can plan their financial arrangements accordingly and know when they will get the keys to the property. In relation to payment of funds to your solicitor, there are three key stages.

Firstly, there is money on account with your solicitor to go towards your legal fees and third-party disbursements payable during the conveyancing. This will usually be requested at the outset when you sign your solicitor's terms of business and they commence working on your property purchase. It is normally around £500 and will cover disbursements such as the usual property searches and any Land Registry official copies or searches made. Some solicitors will not request money on account and you should find out this information prior to signing any terms of business.

The second payment of funds to your solicitor is usually made just before exchange of contracts for the deposit. This is normally 10% of the agreed purchase price, or such other amount agreed between you and your seller to constitute the deposit on exchange. Your solicitor will request the transfer of deposit funds to their client account when both parties are ready to exchange contracts.

The final payment of funds to your solicitor is just before completion. Your solicitor will provide you with a statement of account noting the legal fees, as well as disbursements already incurred or to be paid following completion, and request the final balance funds from you to complete the sale. If you are purchasing with mortgage finance, your solicitor will require the stamp duty funds to be transferred at this point too, and this figure will be included in your statement of account also. The final balance funds will need to be in your solicitor's client account prior to completion, so they can transfer the full balance purchase price to the seller on the agreed completion date.

Question 6: 'Can you give some top tips for getting the most out of your solicitor?'

Firstly, be proactive. If you are proactive, your solicitor is more likely to be proactive also. This is because they will see that you are keen and willing to help as much as possible and your interests are aligned – to get you moved into your new property as per your target timeframe. So, for example, if you have a telephone conversation, do follow up with an email detailing your discussion and confirming what you have agreed to do to keep things moving on your side – it may be that your solicitor provides this follow-up email themselves.

Either way, it is important that both you and your solicitor can clearly see what was discussed and agreed, so there is no confusion and it is clear that you understand the advice and information provided to you. You could also agree a follow-up timeframe each time to ensure some time is booked in already, which keeps up the momentum and confirms when you can expect to hear further. When both solicitor and buyer are on the same page and working together, the process is less stressful, more enjoyable and much quicker to completion.

Secondly, let your solicitor know any important information such as any planned holidays, babies due, school registration or school holiday timeframes when you will be less available or anything else that is coming up that may impact your ability to communicate or be involved in the conveyancing process. It may be that you must complete the purchase before a certain date and, if not met, you would need to withdraw. It is crucial that information is provided from the outset so that your solicitor can advise you appropriately and work with you to make sure key dates are targeted. You can also ask your solicitor the same and find out about anything planned on their side that may impact your timeframes too. This gives you both an opportunity to plan ahead and make sure you know who to contact at any point. Plans can change throughout the conveyancing process and adjustments can, of course, be made but at least there will be an understanding from the beginning as to what the plan is likely to look like until completion.

Thirdly, setting up a new 'home' email account – whether buying on your own, with a partner or together with others – could save lots of time and hassle during the conveyancing process and also after completion. Often, emails can be missed or unread in between general or junk emails to the usual account or, if purchasing jointly or together with others, forgetting to include all email accounts in the email causes a problem or time delays. Think about a scenario of four friends purchasing together, requesting their solicitor to copy in all of their personal and work email addresses for any information to be provided (this happens!) – the solicitor would spend half their time adding all eight email addresses to the email instead of spending that time writing the same. With a new 'home' email account for all purchasers to access, you can see when emails have been read by all and you will also be receiving a lot less general or junk email, so will be less likely to miss any important emails. It is also an opportunity to clear out the clutter from your usual email account and set up new utilities and billing information to the new 'home' email account on completion, which keeps everything home-related in one place now.

Wills

When buying a property, if you don't already have one, it is a very good idea to get a will.

I asked Victoria Lykke-Dahn, Estate Planning Associate at Radcliffe & Newlands Estate Planning (RNEP), to comment on the subject of wills for first-time buyers.

The need for a will is so much more important when looking to purchase a house. And here's why:

- Without one, it will take your family months and months of stress and hard work to sort out your affairs. It will also cost them quite a lot of money just to establish the right to even start sorting everything out.

- If you're married or civil partners, your spouse or partner doesn't automatically get everything unless you have a will.
- If you're living with someone, your partner gets nothing unless you have a will.
- Do you want to let the government decide who gets what of yours? If the answer is "no", then get a will.
- Do you have friends you would like to leave things to? This isn't possible without a will.
- And finally, a will isn't for ever – it's for now. Wills can be changed as your life changes.

Victoria and her team can be reached on enquiries@rnestateplanning.com, Tel: 0207 3820446.

Remember to go to www.scottrawlings.co.uk for lots of additional free resources and my free podcast containing plenty of additional help.

Glossary

APRC – Annual Percentage Rate of Charge. This shows the total cost for the mortgage taking into account the interest rate charged, the variable rate in the future, and any additional costs.

Arrangement Fee – Also known as a booking fee, completion fee. A fee charged by the mortgage lender for the pleasure of borrowing money from them.

Base rate – The Bank of England rate of interest on which many banks base their mortgage pricing.

Cashback – Some mortgage products offer a cashback to help with costs (such as £250 towards legal fees.)

Completion – The point at which the property transaction is completed and you get the keys.

County Court Judgement (CCJ) – If you default on the debt, that judgement will be registered on your credit file and will affect your ability to borrow money.

Deeds – The formal written document which details who legally owns a property.

Disbursements – Expenses that form part of the legal costs. These will include paying for searches or paying to transfer monies.

Exchange of contracts – The point at which a purchase becomes legally binding between a buyer and a seller. It is also the point that deposit monies become payable.

Key Facts Illustration (KFI) – A document from the mortgage lender that gives all the facts and figures for the mortgage.

Land Registry – Government body that holds details of land and property ownership.

LISA – Lifetime ISA.

LTV – Loan to Value. The size of your mortgage compared to the property value. If you are putting down a 10% deposit, this gives you a 90% LTV.

Negative Equity – If a property value falls below the current mortgage balance, that is known as negative equity.

Payment holiday – Some mortgage products allow you to take a short break from making your mortgage payments.

Portability – Refers to the ability to move your mortgage product to a new property should you wish to move house.

Redemption Penalty – A fee charged by a mortgage company should the mortgage be paid off within a certain period. For example, if you take out a five-year fixed rate mortgage and pay it off within those five years, you may be charged a fee. This is typically between 3% and 5% of the loan amount.

Residence nil rate band – Additional relief within inheritance tax should part of your estate be made up of residential property.

Self-build mortgage – A type of mortgage that allows you to use the money loaned to build a property. Normally, the money is loaned at various stages of the build process.

Acknowledgements

Sachin is a good friend and client and when I told him my plan to write a book he suggested that I read *The Miracle Morning by Hal Elrod*. I highly recommend this book if you want to get things achieved in a short amount of time. As a result of reading this book, I was able to finish my book in record time, whereas previously I had been stalling due to lack of time for many months.

Many thanks also to my contributors – Fiona, Victoria and Hannah – truly awesome people who know their stuff.

Christian Lennon has helped me massively. He is simply a marketing genius and has the most awesome way with words and has taught me loads about writing.

Jason Ransted recruited me into the financial services industry over 20 years ago and has been my mentor and good friend ever since. He gave me the knowledge and inspiration to go out there and educate first-time buyers. Thank you Jason.

My big sis, Tracy Littlejohn, for all the help typing up my notes.

Carl Welham – truly nice guy and expert at this literary malarkey.

My good friend Carl Gilbert – the nicest guy ever, who is always willing to give his time to help others – thanks Carl.

Stephanie Hale – introduced to me by a property investor and I couldn't ask for a more awesome publisher. And actually that property investor – Tim Matcham – gave me the inspiration for the title of this book, so thank you Tim.

And finally my wife Sarah. I cannot explain here just how much she has supported me over the years but in a word – she is a amazing x (Is that more than one word?)

SOURCES

https://www.legalandgeneral.com/bank-of-mum-and-dad/bomad-report-2019.pdf

https://www.bbc.co.uk/news/business-47070020 – average age of first-time buyers

http://www.swanlowpark.co.uk/savings-interest-data – savings rate source

https://www.finder.com/uk/personal-loans-statistics – loan rate source

ABOUT THE AUTHOR

Scott has over 20 years' experience helping first-time buyers and believes passionately in sharing his knowledge to help as many people as possible. He speaks regularly at events up and down the country and has convinced many HR directors to provide education for first-time buyers as part of their employee benefits and well-being initiatives in the workplace. The attendees leave his events with a clear understanding of the buying process and what they need to do to get on the property ladder.

Scott lives near Basingstoke, Hampshire, with his wife Sarah and two children Isabelle and Ben – both of whom (he has no doubt) he will help at some point to get on the property ladder in some way or another. But that's a little way off as Ben is 10 and Izzy is 12.

If you want to get in touch with Scott, then head over to www.scottrawlings.co.uk.

Printed in Great Britain
by Amazon

63439059R00066